The Perfect Image
of an
Imperfect World

TEN 19 MEDIA GROUP

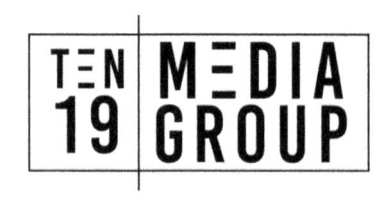

The Perfect Image of an Imperfect World

Written by: Chantel Walls
Editor: Christina Berard, B.A., M.S., LCDP
Photography by: Sheree Omodunbi

Copyright ©2018 Chantel Walls

ISBN-13: 978-1986280396
ISBN-10: 198628039X

For booking, scheduled appearances and more visit
www.ChantelWalls.com

All rights reserved. This book or any portion thereof may not be reproduced or used in any manner whatsoever without the expressed written permission of the author except for the use of brief quotations in a book review.

Ten19 Media Group
P.O. Box 4454
Tampa, FL 33677
ten19mediagroup@gmail.com

Printed in the United States of America

I dedicate this book in memory of my grandmother Louise R. Singleton, my mother Gale Walls and my father Paul Walls.

I am ever most grateful to my grandmother, who was very intelligent, witty and adventurous. If it had not been for her I would not be able to express myself through my writings and words. I remember my first notebook given to me was from my grandmother. In this notebook, I would write any and everything. We would sit down together and write short stories, poetry, songs, etc.

This was something I held so near and dear to my heart because it allowed me to express myself without judgement or criticism.

My mother, Gale Walls, a woman of elegance, strong-will and intelligence possessed many talents. I wish to be half the woman my mother was. Through all the hard times, she still managed to smile. She protected like a lion protects her cub. My mother understood me in ways that others did not. She accepted and understood that I was introverted. She understood that when I smiled, I still held worries and pain. We completed each other. The day that she passed away my heart broke. I remember praying and asking God for her to hold on. My mother instilled in me that it was ok to dream; it was ok to be who I am. She wanted me to live my life.

Although my father and I had little time together, I thank him for creating me and loving me the best way he could. I was daddy's little girl. He pulled me around in my red wagon and he taught me how to ride my bike. The last time I saw him, after so many years, was like a scene out of a movie. In the middle of the train station, I was still able to pick him out of the crowd

I want to thank my family for holding me, supporting me, loving me, and telling me I can do anything. A special thanks to my aunt Susan for being more than an aunt. She is my best friend and more importantly, took the role of my mother. My friends, thank you for being there through it all. Thank you to my church family for prayers, support, and being my family away from home.

> I want to give encouragement and hope to the world.

Please believe that life is worth living.

No matter the hardship, trials or circumstances, continue through the process, and learn your identity. Through it all lies beauty.

You are the perfect image in this imperfect world.

Table of Contents

HOPE

Perfect Image of an Imperfect World....11

A Friend is He....13

Captured by Hope....15

Listen to your Heart....17

Peace of Mind....19

Perfect Storm....21

The Light upon my Path....23

Time....27

True Love....29

Where Would You Be?....31

FAITH

All Life Matters....35

Blessings....37

Jeremiah 29:11....39

Father Forgive Me....41

Independence....43

In Him I am Me....45

Invincible....47

Keep your Faith...49

Peace Be Still...51

Spirit Guide....55

2 Timothy 1:7....57

(CONTINUED)

(TABLE OF CONTENTS CONTINUED)

REMEMBRANCE

A Letter to My Earthly Father....61

Beautiful Queens...65

Born Royally....69

Isaiah 54:17....71

Triumphant Beauty....73

DREAM

Beyond the Wilderness....77

Dear Diaries...79

Road to Success....81

Life's Ocean....83

Nature of People....87

Open Heart Surgery....91

The Bigger Picture....95

Your Book has Already Been Written....97

Victor and Victim....101

Victim vs Victor....103

The Perfect Image of an Imperfect World

Hope

Perfect Image of an Imperfect World

When you look in the mirror
Who is it that you see?
Is it the person that you always wanted to be?
What is the image that you perceive?
I hope it's the image that you care to be

See we all get criticisms every day
Society seems to dictate the way
The way we need to look
The way we need to dress
Yet society can't clean up their mess

Is that who you want to be?
I need you to stand alone
Stand alone for what you believe in
And continue the fight within
No one can determine who you are for
We are all made in God's image

A Friend is He

Where can I go when I feel alone?
Who do I turn to when my skies are grey?
What is it that I do when I can no longer feel what I say?
I tell you, my child, your worries are no longer

You have Friend that will cover
For He has heard your cries
He has wiped your tears away
He has walked with you in all your steps
He is Jehovah, shadow in the depths
He has been where you have
And he has cleared your path
He taught you along the way
He is the one that guides you on this journey
He has left words for us to meditate on
He has been there all along

The Friend I have in him is always constant
The best friendship that is everlasting
He has loved me, when I didn't love myself

He wept when I couldn't
I wanted to give up
He graciously loved me when I turned a blind eye

What a beautiful friend

He has showed me what peace means

He's the replica we need to be

He is perfect in all his ways, but still asked His Father to forgive him

He was tempted like us, but He heard His Father's voice

I need this Friend in me

What a beautiful Friend is He

Captured by Hope

Every time I sit and think
I can never let my mind be free
My thoughts are so jumbled they confuse me
I try and try to believe, and sometimes I can only disagree
Is this where life is taking me?

Bound to the chains of my inner most thoughts
Always feeling left in the dark
Are the choices I make in life right?
I just want to be brought to the light

What more can I do to feel so accomplished?
Where everyone can be astonished,
Astonished at the decisions I've made
The success being displayed

Without anyone being dismayed
Why do I look to others that don't know me?
I want to be known for what I do, my work's so true
The passion that burns inside to share with other eyes

Will that make me satisfied
I want more out of life
Not to deal with strife
But society has me believe that I can be free

How can I be free if social status won't let me?
Where we all compete for the same things
Money and wealth were hands we all weren't dealt
And yet I still sit and think

Well is it just me ?

The world that we exist in
Nothing will ever change in an instant
Yet I'm still tortured by my thoughts
Society has a say on how successful I will be

But won't give me a chance to let me be me

I shouldn't live by society's rules
The world is so cruel
I shouldn't care what others think of me
I'm going to live life to the best of my ability

I'm going to take all my thoughts and crumble them up
Make them to believe I will be something someday
To their dismay

I'm going to live for myself and nobody else
And anyone who doesn't like the decisions I make
I'm sorry to say

But you have just become the contradictions within the world today

Listen to Your Heart

Listen to your heart
What does is it say?
Mine listens to the adversities of today

Listen to your heart
What does it beat?
Mine beats for every child that's taken away

Listen to your heart
What does it cry?
Mine cries loud despairing pride

Listen to your heart
What do you feel?
Mine feels for every mother that loses her child in the streets

Stop and look deep down inside
Pushing away that pride
Look at what's going on around you
Listen to the cries

What is it that you can do
To make someone else's day
Whether it's a Hi or a Hug
You have just made a way

Stop and think of what you have
That others may not
Be grateful for each day
Because when you look away
Someone has just lost the fight for today

Even though we all go through
Count your blessings to
Keep them close to your heart
Never depart

So what does your heart really say?
Are you going to be the difference of today?

Perfect Storm

They say, "when it rains it pours"
And then the thunder roars
But in the eye of tragedy
There's something more

The clouds will part
The sun will peek through
You will see the Rainbow
This is God's promise to you

Just know his newness inside
Will likely collide
With the beauty on the outside
So stand with pride

You have made it through the worst
Don't be afraid to boast
Because when the storm broke
the glass in
You picked up the pieces

When the wind whirled
You held on
Now this is what I call a Perfect Storm

Peace of Mind

I smile because I'm happy
A glow within me has arrived
I am more than what you see on the outside
My beauty comes from the inside

Simplicity makes me unique
I'll set myself apart from the rest

For this person that is before you
has knowledge of the struggle
But my smile...

My smile emulates the meaning of
true happiness
For this is my peace of mind

The Light Upon My Path

Dear Lord,

My heart feels hardened and tears I can no longer cry

"He heals the brokenhearted and binds up their wounds"

Psalms 147:3

Lord, I feel I can't go on, it has all become too much, where do I go from here?

"So do not fear, for I am with you; do not be dismayed, for I am your God. I will strengthen you and help you; I will uphold you with my righteous right hand"

Isaiah 41:10

But Lord, I can't stand to hear what people say about me, they always judge me and talk behind my back,

"No weapon formed against thee shall prosper; and every tongue that shall rise against thee in judgement thou shalt condemn. This is the heritage of the servants of the Lord, and their righteousness is of me, saith the Lord"

Isaiah 54:17

I feel so depressed and suppress everything deep down inside, it consumes my mind.

"Put on the whole armor of God, that ye may be able to stand against the wiles of the devil"

Ephesians 6:11

Lord Jesus, give me understanding to know who I am in you. I know that you know what I go through, I just don't know where I am anymore. I feel worthless

My Child,

"You were made in my image"

> Genesis 1:27

"Before I formed you in the womb I knew you, before you were born I set you apart; I appointed you as a prophet to the nations"

> Jeremiah 1:5

"You are fearfully and wonderfully made"

> Psalm 139:14

"For I know the plans I have for you, plans to prosper you not to harm you; plans to give you a hope and a future"

> Jeremiah 29:11

God, what is it that I'm supposed to do, who is it that you want me to be? Why do the things that happen, happen to me? I'm afraid of the life I live.

"Whomever you may approve, I will send them letters to carry your gifts to Jerusalem"

> I Corinthians 16:3

"For God hath not given us the spirit of fear, but of power and love and a sound mind"

> 2 Timothy 1:7

Ok Lord, but what about financial situations? It just seems to pile up. Another thing I can't leave to rest

"Therefore do not be anxious, saying what shall we eat or what shall we drink, or what shall we wear? For the Gentiles seek after all these things, and your Heavenly Father knows that you need them all; but seek first the kingdom of God and righteousness and all these things will be added to you. Therefore, do not be anxious about tomorrow for tomorrow will anxious for itself. Sufficient for the day is its own trouble"

> Matthew 6:31-34

My God, you are the light upon my path,

You have brought me through the darkness

I can smile brighter because I feel your comfort

I can finally see past all my pain; your love is what I gain

"I am crucified with Christ: nevertheless I live ye not I, but Christ liveth in me; and the life which I now live in the flesh, I live by the faith of the Son of God, who loved me and gave himself for me"

Galatians 2:20

You are the light upon my path

The lamp upon my feet

I shall no longer live in darkness

You shall live in me

Please guide me in the darkest time

Even then the light will shine

You have shown me greater

I know you are not against me

Be the light upon my path

The lamp upon my feet

Thank you for sending the Risen King

Time

I can't turn back the hands of time even if I tried
I want to go back to where things felt safe
Where it all took place

A place where things were golden
Even though I was chosen
I was chosen on a path, that God knew I could withstand

I want to turn back the hands of time
Just to remember what it was like
What it felt like to laugh again

To smile ear to ear
To feel joy and no fear
I fear for things that may be headed my way
I've wasted enough time so to say

I wish there was enough time to say everything I wanted
Enough time to not feel haunted
By the worries of my inner most thoughts

I wish I could turn back the hands of time
to undo what has already been done
To fix things and not run

There's never enough time to get all that you want
But the time that you do have
Keep it near and dear to your heart

True Love

I've never felt a love so true
A love that follows through
A love that can grace me with it's presence each and everyday
A love that will never fade away
This kind of love is rare
The kind of love I want to be able to share
The kind of love I can grow to have
Only if I follow the path that was chosen for me
The kind of love that can reach down to the depths of my soul
I've never felt this kind of love
That emulates from the sun
The way it's so heart felt and warm
I can just bask in this love because
Of the golden rays and the warmness that I can feel
A true love that I don't have to go searching for because It was already given
The kind of love that doesn't make me feel imprisoned
The kind of love where I wake up and sing
A love where my heart skips a beat
The kind of love where my breath is taken away
The kind of love where it's hard to say how I really feel
And all I can do is cry to express the joy within
A love that came straight from above
A love that came shining down from Heaven
The love that God showed me even then

He sacrificed his only son to give me new life
All I can do is give glory to that choice
So I shall give the true love back
And it shall never lack
Because my love should be on the same level as His
My praise and worship shall never be the same because I know I fall short of His grace
But through it all, his love comes bursting through
And when I call, he hears and it will pull me through
This true love is hard to find because this love is Heavenly Divine
The kind of love I can feel within my Spirit, now I can declare it
Thank you Heavenly Father for your love in the truest form
Your love holds me through the storms
Your love helps me through it all
Your love helped me hear your call
Your love in its glorious, magnificent view

Thank you for your true love you allow me to continuously receive it

Where Would You Be? (Dedicated to John 3:16)

There's always going to be a time in your life when you feel down and out

When no one will understand your struggle

The things that are happening seem unrealistic

And you can't grasp the concept of why things ae happening to you

But I ask you

Where would you be if you weren't going through tough situations?

Where would you be if everything was perfect?

Where would you be if you had everything you wanted?

Where would you be if all your wishes were granted?

Where would you be if you handled everything on your own?

Where would you be if the ones that said they loved you stayed?

Where would you be if all your financial situations changed?

Where would you be if you didn't have the one's that cared for you so much?

Where would you be if God's grace didn't save you from so much?

Where would you be if your job wasn't going through a lot?

Where would you be without His love, peace, and Joy?

There are certain things we ask God for and we think he doesn't hear us

But the reality is he has already granted us

Where would we all be without His son Jesus?

He died for us and our sins on The Cross
Where would we all be if this didn't take place?
The pain that He suffered was for me and you
And the things we go through; there shouldn't be an excuse

So I ask, where would you be without all the experiences you go through
Your situations help you in the long run
Even though they can be rough,
God's grace is enough

It's enough to know that you will get through because he has already made a plan for you
Talk to God all the time
He will hear you and bring you out

Thank God for the harder times; he makes your smile brighter

Pray to him about it all
He will answer your call
And he will reveal things to you that can't be seen just yet
Listen to the voice that is in your head
That's God answering your prayers
Where would you be?

Faith

All Life Matters

You are bold
You are beautiful
You are all that you were created to be

Understandably,
Life gets tough
The feeling is to give up

You may have even felt you weren't good enough
Disparity and fear have a control
Along with other feelings deep in your soul

I just want to say,
Your life matters to all those around you
You are unique in your own special way

Please look deep inside your heart
God hears your thoughts
Don't think that things won't change
You will never find out if you take your life away

Give life a chance
It is really worth living
God has created a purpose for your life

That is what he is all about
He doesn't kill. He brings forth new life
Your life truly matters
This is a fact
You could be that inspiration for someone else to be exact

Look deep inside and re-evaluate your situation
I guarantee things will come into fruition

Your life truly matters
This I tell you so
Even when you don't love yourself
God will love you more...

Be humbled in the presence of the
Lord
Excellence is what He represents; His
Soothing touch reaches the depths of my
Soul; He
Ignites the flames I have to praise Him
Nurturing is His Holy Spirit
Gracious is His love; He always
Sends His Angels in protection from above

Dedicated to Jeremiah 29:11

"For I know the plans I have for you",
declares the Lord,
"Plans to prosper you, not harm you,
plans to give you hope and a future."

Sometimes you look to the sky and ask why
Why do the hardships I go through seem to come upon more?
You know what they say, "when it rains it pours"
You go through the days straying away
Thinking you can handle it alone and it will go away

And as you take it day by day
Nothing seems to go away

It consumes your mind and heart like a toxic poison
And still your spirit is loitering
But when everything becomes too much to bare
The Lord is always there

For he was waiting for you with open arms
No more need to feel alone
He knew you were going to come to him
But waited until you found it within

Found it in within yourself the strength to walk in faith
And now that you've built up your faith
Your spirit becomes safe

The Lord never leaves us alone for he has had a plan all along
Count your blessings everyday
He promised to never leave you astray
And even when you feel like he isn't there
Listen to your spirit

It declares all the truths that lie within
This proves the trust you have with him
Continue to pray each and every day he gives you the power of prayer

And when things begin to change,
Know that it was all within God's plan
He is the one we believe in for hope and the future

He is the one we believe in for hope and the future
For we are all his children

He loves us in each and every way
And he will protect us every day

Father Forgive Me

Hello Father, I know that you **hear me**
I feel your presence everywhere I go
Especially when I'm talking to you
You give me your precious **Holy Spirit**
When I look in the mirror I no longer see **a broken girl**
I see a **young woman made** in the image you created me to be

Father, I have to continuously ask for your **forgiveness**
because I'm not perfect
At several points in time I felt **so lost** and had **no idea** where to go or what to do

I went to others for answers; but my questions were never answered
While trying to get what I thought I needed,
I was spending money to get **a piece of mind**
Still, I couldn't find the **perfect image** of myself in this **imperfect world**

Through it all, you **favored me**

I fell down, but you picked me up and put my feet on solid ground
I had to truly **give myself away** and **withhold nothing** from you

You helped me to stand strong

I could have never *imagined myself* where I am now

Filled with nothing but your peace and love

I *know true love* because you allowed me to *break every chain*

It's just *because of who you are* that I'm thankful for the ability to receive your *blessings*

Father, forgive me for turning my back on you all those times

indescribable is truly who you are

Thank you for giving me *the equations* I needed to bare my crosses

I thank you for redirecting my path

Your protection told me that *no weapon will be formed against me*

And this I believe with all my heart

My Prince of Peace, you give me all I need to survive

Father please forgive me, I had no idea how much I was hurting *you*

Where would I be? You are the constant friend this world needs

You teach me what victory truly means

Father, please forgive me

I am strong
Nothing can
Defeat me,
Except me. I can
Propel forward in
Exceptional ways
Noticing this makes me brave
Doing what makes me happy is what matters
Eager to see what comes my way
Nudging away those who have nothing nice to say
Trusting my instincts in many ways

In Him I am Me

I am strong
I am bold
I am everything He created me to be
I am unique
I am creative
In his ways I am loved.

Yes, I can be afraid
I can be betrayed
I can be self-conscious
These are just spirits that get in the way

No, I am not perfect
I have made my mistakes
All lessons I learned in life

I'd rather stand out and lead
Than be popular and follow
I dare to be different because I am me

I am the image that God sees

Ignorance is the ways of the flesh
Noticing this, you are
Victorious, you are complete
In the way God wants you to be
Never allow others to have
Control over your life
It will never be worth the strife
Be all you can be because The
Lord will
Excel you abundantly

Keep Your Faith

When I think about Faith and Obedience
A wave comes upon me
I think about how my Faith will set me free
I think about how my Lord will work through me

I think about where I was versus where I am now
See I thought I was handling it all
God was only teaching me to crawl
But I was still rushing to get somewhere...

Didn't realize that I still needed him to walk
Each time I got up, I would fall
Still didn't realize he was breaking my fall
Telling me, "My child just wait on me and continue to crawl."

I was getting hasty and still didn't want to wait
I wanted everything fast to heal my heartache
I heard a whisper in my ear,

"My child I am here; just crawl
Just wait on me, I will heal
My strength and power prevails"

Even though I heard this whisper,
Things weren't moving quicker

Thinking I knew what was right
I put myself in a pit
One deeper than before
Once again I heard his voice

"My Child, I am here
Please have no fear"
I felt comfort knowing he was there
This time I bowed down and listened

I'm only going to crawl
For when He is ready, I will then be ready to walk
At first, I didn't believe that I would pull through
But his love pulled me through

So, when you think about God's love

Truly think about what he does
How is it that he is more OBEDIENT to us
Than we are to him?

But that's the thing his love is never ending
keep the FAITH
Never depart from his grace
For his love is everlasting

And salvation received from him is better than committing your life to sins
Commit your Life to him

Keep your Faith

Peace Be Still

I'm the soldier and the
plain that is existing in is called the battle field of life

The constant fight with the enemy
Because he always wants a piece me
Trying to take what's mine
But all I'm trying to do is survive

See, like the soldier, I'm only trained in a certain specialty
called reality
And in reality, I have to learn and grow
But the enemy will always deter me
Because he's afraid of
the success that I will be

Just like with any battle it started with a conflict
So you make a plan to resolve it
When two parties can't agree
It can only help me to believe
That the enemy won't let me free

Now I'm stuck in between the fight for
Good and Evil
I have to stand my ground to retrieve my territory
this is the plain that the enemy is standing on
In order to counteract what the enemy is doing
I have to go war

I have to drop everything else around me
To free the battlefield
To release the negativity and let it peacefully be filled

Like a soldier, I'm scared for what's about to be done
I have to get my protection but not using guns
Instead I get suited up with the armor of God
His protection will be my weapon

I'm fully equipped to go to war
God's words are my sword
Shots fired

Guns drawn; the enemy is coming strong

I wasn't ready for what the enemy came to do...

So I hide, thinking I can't make it through
I sulk in my own pain
Now I'm sitting
Feeling like I can't be saved

For a moment, I let the enemy win this fight
Because I can't deal with this life
I'm on this battlefield
And don't want to fight

The enemy is taking control of me
And I let him
Because there's no other way to be
At least from what I can see
But something dawns on me

See, the enemy has conspired with my flesh
He's taking me through this mess
But it wasn't only him alone. My flesh connected to my soul,
allowed for it to be controlled
So the shots fired weren't just anything unusual
It was coming from what was deeply rooted in my soul

It was part of me
It was my flesh
I am my worst enemy
I became one with the enemy
I couldn't achieve what God has planned for me

Again I'm the soldier
And I'm getting ready for war
So I put the armor of God on and ask for more
But I didn't need to because God was there all along

Shots fired
Guns drawn

I tried to dodge, but God said to stand strong
"Peace be with you"
And "peace be still"

'No weapons formed against you shall prosper"
You better claim this battlefield

I stood strong with my protection and armor on
Next thing I know, the enemy started missing
he couldn't handle it at all

I looked to my left and I looked to my right
I no longer see the flesh
I see spiritual light

I no longer became my worst enemy
it just came to be
that the actual enemy
brainwashed me

Standing in this battlefield of life
The enemy is weakened because I'm not the only soldier putting
on the armor of God

With each soldier standing strong
The enemy is weakened and falls

We are the soldiers that God sent on earth to fight
we fight with peace and spiritual light
we claim back the territory that the enemy tried to take
But in the end God has the final say

The battlefield is the situations within the earthly realm
The question is
Are you going to let the enemy score
Or are you going to put the armor of God on
And become Victorious in the war?

Spirit Guide

My spirit is telling me something different
And I can feel it...

It's telling me to stay encouraged
Because I know have the courage
And even when I feel like I don't
I must look to evil and say, "You Won't!"

You won't allow me to feel this way
For devil, you need to go away
Your presence is not wanted here
I suggest you stand clear

You stand clear for what the Lord is about to do
His miracles are so true
The devil can no longer hold me captive
I have the power of action

The action to walk with the Lord
And be active within his word
You shall no longer put me down
For his glory is my crown

You can't take away the happiness from within
It will shine bright like the sun rays
And even if you think you have stripped me of my pride and joy
I will look up and say, "no more!"

I can get down on my knees
And ask my Father, please

Please forgive me of my sins
For he gave His life
And even though I'm not perfect
You still call me your daughter

And to think when I was down and out
I had no more strength to shout
I just wanted it all to end
All I could see was an end

An end of all the pain and hurt
I thought that would solve it all
But then I heard a call

Jesus whispered in my ear and said,
"My child I am here
Let me protect you
And put you in my arms
You will never be alone."
And now I know

I no longer have to feel lost
For the Lord brought me to him
And when I start to feel weak
I get down upon my knees
To let the devil know his presence is never wanted here
I will not fear

I believe in my Lord
And his words are forever my protection and sword

Dedicated to 2Timothy1:7

"For God hath not the spirit of fear; but of power, and of love, and of a sound mind."

The Lord has blessed my heart for I have no fear
My thoughts, my mind so clear
I feel oppression in the days that I walk
But all I can do is talk

Speak the living word that God has put on this earth
For he chose me for rebirth
His glory, his grace have been so amazing
The love I feel is appraised

The power of love shall be spread through me
For the gift I have sets me free

The gifts you give, I have to realize for myself
But you give it to spread to those who need help

Dear Lord, when I have you, I have no fear
For my mind, my soul, and my spirit are free
Be with me, help me to walk in your faith
For I know you will never forsake

Bless my heart for I have no fear
My Lord , My Jesus, My savior is here

Remembrance

A Letter to my Earthly Father

Let me tell you something about a Father's love...
It's something so pure and true a love that has been created since the beginning of time.

A love that stretches and grows like a vine that creates the stems of a rose.
Now, you sit there and think why I said a vine
Now, let me tell you why.

Vines start from seeds
A seed that was planted by a warm heart; a heart that wanted to see it grow and become the beauty that it was meant to be.

Now, I am that seed that was planted years ago. I'm that beauty that the rose on this vine represents
Just like the vine, I needed to be nurtured and cared for. As science proves, it's something called photosynthesis

Just like any plant, it needs the sun and water to grow; coming straight from the earth, a miracle arrives that just doesn't know how to survive on its own.

I'm the miracle that was sent from heaven and you and my mother were the sunlight and the water that I needed to grow

Now in its perfection of beauty, this vine creates something we wouldn't have thought. On this vine are thorns that it knew it was going to produce from growth. See, this is the beauty in God's creations

I needed you as my sunlight to grow and learn; to learn to become the beauty of a budding rose
But little did I even know that you were going to produce thorns.

The thorns on a rose vine are beautiful to look at, but be careful how you touch them. The pain that the thorn produces is like no other. Have you ever wondered why the vine has so many thorns?

Well if you haven't I have....

See the thorns on this vine are its protection from anything that harms it. They are the shields that keep its stem so strong

See, yes you were there to water me; you were there to nurture me, but only for so long.

After a while, this budding rose vine only had one source of sunlight and watering that became a lot for only one nurturer to bare

Why weren't you there?

You were supposed to help nurture and grow and not just plant the seed
You helped produce the thorns that I carried for my protection
These thorns were created from not having you around;

See, you told me I was Daddy's Little Girl
But your actions didn't stand by your words

In the beginning you were my Nurturer; you planted that seed and were there in the beginning
But when you left, the pain was unbearable so you became just a Planter to me
You planted the seed and only nurtured for a period of time, but didn't stay to see the beauty that was being produced.
You caused my thorns...

Even when you left this earth, you were just a planter to me
But as I was seeking God,
I had to think about how he made all creations. Even though he knew what they were going to turn out to be, my stem was weak.
The thorns I produced hurt others and myself

I needed to run back and ask for forgiveness

Because I put the blame on you; my thorns became a protection so strong that I couldn't see other nurturers that God sent here on earth;

I also couldn't see that my Heavenly Father provided Sunlight, Water, The Seed, The Petals, The Soil and everything that I needed to grow because he knew that you weren't able to provide ;

He sent other Nurturers and you were no longer just a Planter

See, you then rose to the occasion until God called you home.

Even though you weren't there to see the vine
or the budding rose, you were able to see the beauty of a fully developed Rose that looked just like you

You got to see the beauty that had fully developed from the miracle that God helped you produce.

I thank you for Being a Nurturer, A Planter,
and a Nurturer again. Even though you are no longer here, I know you are proud of the Rose Vine that you have developed, both good and bad.

Thank You Dad and may you REST IN PEACE

Love Always,

your Beautiful Rose Vine

Beautiful Queens
(Stand on Your Pedestal)

Young Women; All women

Stop what you are doing and take a good look at yourself in the mirror

Look past all the negativity that is surrounding

your atmosphere

Don't let it consume your mind

Let positivity flourish your vine

You are a beautiful queen

This is true indeed

No matter your size or color

God looks at your heart and nothing other

Hold your head up high

Stand strong to our pride

Stand on your pedestal

Don't look at yourself as worthless

You are worth more than diamonds and pearls

You are worth it all

Value yourself first because when you don't, someone will come along the way to tell you a lie

Egotistical beings exist and because of insecurities within themselves

They will tear you down

My beautiful queens you are worth more than being talked down to

Don't allow yourself to be abused

You are more than what he or she may say
"Beauty is in the eye of the beholder"
And anyone who can behold you for who you are is worth keeping

You are God's creation, made in the image of Him

Let me just say this because it seems to be the trend these days
All this slang and lingo seems to be the way to describe a woman these days
You are nobody's "trap queen"
What does that even mean?

From what I can see, when you have established that as a title for yourself you are truly trapped indeed
You're trapped into a label by society's norms
You've become so enslaved into a lifestyle about not caring or even holding yourself to a standard
Ladies, please realize you weren't made to become a label to a man or anyone for that matter
Stop objectifying yourself on social media ; it's like feeding greedy pleasure
Please cover all your treasures
Queens value each other too
It's not only men that can put us through
We, as women, need to stand as one
Jealousy and envy lurks within the cracks
Which inhibits behaviors against one another and causes us to

react

We need to embrace one another
Empowerment is the way to go
Standing firm with God's everlasting word

What does it mean to truly be a Queen?
By definition, Queen means "a female ruler of an independent state of mind;
One who inherits the position by right of birth"

Ladies did you hear that?

What it means to be a Queen:
When you have an independent state of mind you cannot be controlled
By right of birth, you are truly deserving
You were made a queen you were born royally
Women. treat one another as Queens
Men treat women like queens
My beautiful Queens, made from the ribs of man,
We are equal
No one male or female is higher than the other
We are Kings and Queens of God

My Queens, born royally to the Kingdom of God
No matter your color, ethnicity, or size

Come into your birth right and know who you are
Stand on your pedestal and claim what's yours

Born Royally

You were never a mistake
As most people like to say,
You were never an "oops"
God planned it this way

Your birthday is marked by the day that you were officially sent to earth
God's gift is your birth
You were knitted and created in your mother's womb
God wouldn't plan you a life of gloom

No matter how you came on this earth, you were born royally
You were born to King and Queen ,whom are Royalty
True royalty is what you are, just like the stars in the sky sitting high
You can still rise above all the stigmatisms against you because they aren't true

Your name was already handpicked by the Highest of the Highs
So don't think you were meant to experience the lowest of the lows
Born royally, created to be Kings and Queens of God's Kingdom

You are beautiful
You are bold and strong
you are whomever God created you to be
God created you Royally

Dedicated to Isaiah 54:17

"No weapon that is formed against thee shall prosper; and every tongue that shall rise against thee in judgement thou shalt condemn. This is the heritage of the servants of the Lord, and their righteousness is of me, saith the Lord"

Why do you hurt me with your words
For other ears to be heard?
Why do you bring me down
Instead of build me up?

It's bad enough I listen to the negativity within myself
Why can't we watch each other succeed
Without jealousy and greed?

When those words come into play
There will never be a way to stop the hate
Rise against what others may say
That will be the key that unlocks the gate

Everything else going on in the world
Makes me want to crawl into a ball
The killings, the shootings, innocent lives being taken
Oh, I'm sorry I must be mistaken

Because gangs and groups are the way to go
"They're a family; they help you grow"
That's Satan talking
And you're following his lead, but when God enters you must take the lead
Become the leader he wants you to be

It will never be easy because people will judge
But they are not your judge
They can't condemn you with their words
If you just look up and believe
Ask God to reprieve for those that have done you wrong

"For they know not what they do"
But when you're a child of God he will come through
Some people will never want to see you prosper
It's not your concern to care what others may think of you

You should only focus on what God has in store
For he promised to give it all

Triumphant Beauty

Your Triumphant Beauty came into this world
Like a roaring lion
yet your soul was as gentle as a lamb

Never wanted to hurt anyone just always wanted to give when
you could
You were such a blessing to others
I don't even think you realized

Always a smile on your face
Your every day was a surprise
Your talent reached across the world
You touched many lives

Your intelligence touched the depths of people's souls
including mine
You are always my inspiration
this is true
Don't think that I have forgotten you

You told me I was never alone
And I feel you in my soul
What more can I say?

You were just the epitome
of what a Mother's Love should be
You taught me
molded me
into a little you

It wasn't all perfect
But that's when you stood strong

Having to give away your own
Just to be where you wanted
That is a Mother's love that can't be taunted

God sent you down to care for me
Then he said your work was done
So rest with him
I love you, **Gale Walls**

I know the angels are rejoiced when you were sent down from Heaven to Earth
And I know they sang and rejoiced for your rebirth

I love you forevermore, Mother
And continue to watch over me
As my angel I know you're protecting me

Your triumphant beauty graced this earth on July 12, 1954
And your elegant soul reached the Heavenly realm
gallantly
on April 26, 2011

Dream

Beyond the Wilderness

Escaping to feel safe and secure
I find my special campground to set up my tent here
Unpacking all that I have; I start my wooden fire

Sitting, glaring up at the stars
I bask in the quiet night
Reminiscing on all my experiences and enjoying the peace of mind

Tranquility is what I have now
It hasn't always been this way
To get to my beloved campground, I endured some wildfires

They came quicker and stronger than I thought
The more water I used to put them out
The more it would make the fires burst out

Many times, I wanted to just let the fires take over
I would then become extinct
I wouldn't see what I would be able to produce

Beyond the wilderness there lies a quiet forest
Beyond the wilderness there is intimate beauty
The beautiful trees that create oxygen, give me life

Explicit simplicity of how when it rains the plants and trees grow more

The pouring rain in the forest

Pushes me deeper in thought

Although the animals hibernate,

They are always prepared for what's to come next

No fear or worry in wilderness

Beyond the wilderness is peace

Chirping of the birds and crickets makes a beautiful song

Music to my ears

Mother nature has her beauty and through all the storms

She produces so many feelings

There is joy

Joy of comfort

Joy of laughter

Joy for victory

Joy in wilderness

Before getting to the beloved campground

Traveling through the wilderness

Wilderness of pain, depression, hate and doubt

Because all of that doesn't compare to the beauty you will see

Beyond the wilderness

Dear Diaries

I meticulously write this to you because at times, my heart can be full and confused

Often times, I just don't know what to do or where to go from here.

Writing to you is my outlet;

When I am at a point where I can't tell anyone my inner most thoughts, I rest assured that you hold my deepest, darkest secrets. In you, I experience all my joys and pains

Day by day, I come to you for the littlest things and I know you won't judge or give me shame

Dear Diary, it's like you are my best friend

I can take you wherever I go; writing to you from the depth of my soul. When my mind seems so scrambled, I have clarity within you. I am just free expressively

Everything that I have withheld inside just pours out into you and through my pen. You have become my saving grace time and time again. I must say, as much as I love you, I have not always been faithful.

I know I tend to get so involved in work and make every excuse. I then say maybe not today but the next day. After saying that over and over, the days have now gone by and no entries have been made. I guess that makes you feel forgotten; like I may not care. That is far from the truth.

Diary you have a purpose for me. I come to you because you are my heart. I know that you will never go astray and never forget the days.

We are connected at the hip because you are with me wherever I go. You know what I love the most? love that you are not hypocritical but convict me of my feelings when needed. That is a relationship we have.

You want to know a really funny thing?

Even though it seems like it is just you and me, I am really the third party. Through you, I have a conversation with my Creator.

He makes himself transparent and is the best friend. The one I put all my trust in, my confidant.

He is my Dear Diary

Recovering from
Obstacles in the way
And the wrong turns you may take
Don't allow these to get in our way

Trust your instincts and you will
Overcome what others say

Stay focused in your lane; it is not
Unusual to become distracted, but take a
Crash
Course in
Enthusiasm and learn to try again
Steer your own wheel and you will
Soar in unexplainable ways

Life's Ocean

When you look back at your life
What is it that you truly see?
Do you think about all that you could be?
See I think about life like the sea
The simplicity of beauty
The way the sea just rests day and night
And the calming waves are a beautiful sight

When life is calm it feels so nice
You feel amazing because everything is right
You feel invincible

I just love to see the sunrise on the water,
The sparkling glare is like no other
See, I can only believe that it's God smiling down on me

Everything isn't always going to be calm
At some point the waters are going to be troubled
The waves will be higher
The tide will get stronger
The wind will whirl
Within this perfect storm is a beauty all in it's own

The beauty knowing that it will at some time end

And the sun will come out again
But before that happens, the storm may get stronger
The Ocean will be cold and the sky will be grey
But I guarantee that will change someday

Life is mysterious just like the sea
You can never predict where you will end up
Sometimes you can feel so confused
And have no idea where to look to
At times your heart can be so heavy
Producing such angry waves
And your mind can be mixed, producing harsh winds

In the midst of your life being like the sea
Their again lies the beauty
Your situations produced blessings in disguise
And when it's all over, you will be surprised
The strength that it took to stand and fight the storm

The waters will calm
The winds will settle
The skies will become blue, and the clouds will be puffy white with the sun gleaming on the Ocean

The warmness that you once felt will come again; it couldn't stay perfect
Just like the sea, you had to go deep to find your power and

strength

No matter how the length

I don't know what you may be going through, but I do know what's true

Life is meant to have trials and tribulations, but it's how you handle it to become your revelations

Take the chances and dive into the depths of the sea

Even though you can't swim, you have Protection

I'll take my chances and deal with Life's Oceans

Because I know I'm saved by God's purpose

Nature of People

Seasons are constantly changing because it wasn't meant to stay the same
Weather is so unpredictable; hard to prepare or plan
Something about the seasons changing affects your life drastically
Each time period that passes, turning the clocks ahead or back
Mostly calculating how much sleep you get

The four seasons of life
We, of course, know what they are
Summer, Spring, Winter and Fall
But here's what I would like for you to see
Other than just changing seasons
The seasons represent phases of existence and people will influence it

Spring is considered as the first phase of the year
Raining all the time, but the sun will still shine
As the sunshine occurs, it can all be a blur
Spring allows you to take some action and get involved
It allows you to reflect on it all

Spring is revival, where the birds sing and flowers bloom
The air is fresh and everything seems new
The Rose buds are open and leaves rustle in the winds

People in Spring are not the same
As nature reawakens; there's suddenly a burst of energy
That wasn't felt before
People seem like they are there to stay
As the weather gets better the seasons will once again change
Going into a different phase

Summer, the hottest it will be all year
People take the dare because the weather is warmer
Others start to show their true colors

As the days get longer, they become hotter
The nighttime is hard to rest due to the heat of situations
this shows exactly how people will behave
Just because it's nicer out, everyone has things to do
The moment you need someone, will they be there for you?
Some will stay during the hottest nights and some will
leave just as the heat strikes

Phases of Fall and Winter are almost the same.
The weather gets colder
The birds chirping no longer
The leaves shrivel up and die
The snow shows it's pride
The birds chirping no longer

The leaves shrivel up and die
The snow shows it's pride

People seem to stay when everything is really nice
But once Winter rears its ugly head
Others no longer want to stay during the harshest time of the winter

This is exactly what I want you to see
Beings come and go
Just like the seasons.
Some come in full bloom and help while others produce the deadness that the cold represents

This is just the Nature of People
They constantly change
But the dynamics of character will remain the same

Open Heart Surgery

This table is hard, but here I am
Laying on this cold slab of metal
Unconscious and not having control over what my body feels
These drapes covering what I don't want to see
Oxygen being pumped inside of me
I'm prepped for open heart surgery

My heart damaged and weakened
No longer able to sustain the pressure that its under
Each time my heart pumped of love, I was stabbed by those I thought I could trust
Making it hard to breathe; my lungs seem to fail me

Every expansion of my lungs
My chest pains of deceit take over
My pulse is racing; my head feels light
My arms are getting heavy
I'm having a heart attack
Coming on suddenly
Really wasn't expecting it

My heart weakened more by the lies you have told and the love never shown
The heart can no longer pump the same; the arteries are much too weak

Clogged with all types of stress

Giving chance after chance

My heart can't physically do what my mind wants to

So many circumstances seem to attack the heart

Misinterpretations of love, hurt and deceitfulness

Untrustworthiness, dishonesty, and lack of self-worth seemed to have attacked my heart the worst

Pain is way too much to stay away

I slip into unconsciousness

They said the damage was irreversible

Life can no longer go on; my heart was dead

While unconscious, something is happening

I feel a force taking form I can't really explain

A spiritual light that I have never imagined before

See, people view it as they have broken you so bad you can't come

But God is my ultimate surgeon

He is performing my surgery

He is not going to replace my heart with a new one but instead give me renewal

He is suctioning out all the blood of hurt that initially stabbed me

Next He is repairing the wounds and the walls of my heart by helping me believe in Him

Helping me to learn forgiveness. Even though it hurts, it is part of the process

Clearing my arteries of stress. Casting on my burdens on to him

He begins to take me off bypass and let His work be seen
I can feel my heart begin to beat
I no longer feel shortness of breath
His words implanted in my heart forevermore

Now recovery time begins
Will I pour into other hearts?
So they don't undergo the hurt or pain?

He has opened new opportunities that I couldn't see
I have regained my strength indeed
I will proceed

Once this surgery happened, I could no longer allow the same things to attack my heart
I can't allow the same people to stab me in my chest
My God, My Surgeon won't allow that
Open heart surgery
Such a painful procedure to undergo
Letting go of the old to bring in the new

He hurts the way we hurt because we hurt each other
But He does this procedure to give a new beginning
A life beyond our wildest dreams once you believe

I have a life with a renewed heart
I live a life where I can breathe again
There may be some blocked arteries along the way
But God will clear them out of your path
You have to forgive all the hurt and attacks on the heart by others

I allowed God to open my heart
I now live a life where I know self-worth
I allowed God to open my heart
I now live a life where I know self-worth
I made it through my adversaries
I allowed God to perform my open-heart surgery
Will you allow Him to do yours too?

The Bigger Picture

It's the little moments in life that really count
Snapshot a picture to relive the moment
Not really thinking about what it means

I could look at this picture day in and day out
I'm able to connect it to a memory of heart felt love
Looking at the picture brings me much joy

Until a feeling strikes and I can't enjoy it anymore
I don't want to feel the pain, so I erase the memory
Yet it's still saved in other ways to see

Looking at the bigger picture
It's so much more than you ever thought it could be
That snapshot of your life can teach you a valuable lesson
No matter who or what it is, it happened for a reason

And even though right now it's not plain to see
Someday it will dawn on you when you least expect it
Keep those snapshots even though they hurt
It's the pain that truly helps you learn

Snapshot here and Snapshot there
Keep it near your heart

The bigger picture will be revealed

Your Book Has Already Been Written

So you think your book is done?
There's nothing else to write
No ideas are flowing so you put the pen down

Well, I'm coming to tell you that's not the truth
In reality, your book is just beginning
In actuality, your book has already been written
Everything has already been mapped out
Your ideas were already determined from birth
Once you were born, the plot took place
And the characters were already made

Your book was created from the back to the front,
Giving you the option to write what you want
The message of your book has already been predetermined
But your path is left up to you

The chapters of your book were set
Your book has already been written
The numbers of your pages have already been counted from hundreds to thousands

Your every thought and action has already been attested for
Now are you going to go forth?

Are you going to share your book with others
So they can experience your testimony?
Are you going to create the sequels
To continue what never ends?
Your book has already been written from cover to cover
From introduction to summary

The cover will bring it all together
Whether it matches the message or not, it has been left for you to decide
The creativity that flows within you
will come forth, pick a cover that was meant for you

Your book has already been written from end to the beginning
And from the sequel beginning to end

Your chapters were already named
Your pages were already numbered

Your book has already been written
This I tell you is true
Are you going to let the creativity flow ?
If you be all you can be

You can bind your book together and let it flourish
Just know you are the narrator; give thanks to the Author

Your book has already been written and it will be a #1 seller

Your book has already been chosen by the Publisher

Victor and Victim

What does it mean to be a Victor?
Have you given this thought?
I can think of a number of things

To be a Victor means to overcome
To overcome what the enemy wants you to become
To change your circumstances in a way that takes a great deal of strength

Now, it's easier to be a victim than a Victor. Let me tell you why
To be a victim doesn't require much
All you have to do is simply give up
Give up on all your hopes and dreams

Doubt yourself in every way possible
All you have to do is let others dictate who you are
And trust me, if you let that happen, you will never go far

The Victor works hard and never gives up the fight
The Victor faces any obstacles with a smile because they know it's worth while
It's worth it to see the blessings come your way
It's worth it to learn the lessons along the way

The Victor knows his/her purpose

know it's worth while
It's worth it to see the blessings come your way
It's worth it to learn the lessons along the way

The Victor knows his/her purpose
So they stand strong to protect it
Enemies know that you are protecting that purpose
So, of course everything will be done to stop it
But the Victor sees the battle through

So, which is it that you would like to be?
The victim or the Victor?
Even though God has predestined us
He gives us free will
Remember it's your choice to pick the path

Choose wisely because the way you see your situation will be the outcome

Victor vs. Victim

Victim vs Victor (Part 2)

Ultimately the fight has begun
Once you begin to turn the other cheek
The gloves are put on

Round 1 takes place
You meet your opponent face to face, he
Unknowingly blindfolds you and something comes over you
The fear engages within, leaving you dark and confused
Emptiness of not knowing what to do
The round has ended, and you let the enemy take this one
The score is 0-1

Round 2 begins
And you feel the fight within
Endurance may cover you
As you protect what you may need to
And yet you're stricken with a punch to the gut
The pain from it makes you fall to your knees
But listen to the voice that tells you to get up
Listen to what it says, "Don't give up"
Come back with a *jab* to the face
It doesn't matter what you're fighting against

Hit 'em with the *one/two combo*
Then you hit back to the gut
Now because you fought back
You just caught up with the opponent

1-1

So now you've endured a situation that you were battling against

Now you stand with confidence

But sometimes too much confidence consumes you

You start to think you're untouchable

But each phase is completely different and isn't always apparent

It's now **Round 3**

And you feel fulfilled

Your heart is jumping

Adrenaline is flowing

You now have an *upright stance* and feel invincible

See the problem is we can become too prideful and think nothing can stop us

Little did you know what was waiting around the corner

Suddenly,

Your opponent caught up with a quick *Hook* questioning your **Identity**

In this phase you question yourself and who you are

Don't know what to do or how you're going to survive

Feeling hopeless and lost because you lost who you were

You just faced the most hurtful *cross-hook and jab* that you will ever experience

So now you've lost your **identity** to the world and everything starts ripping apart

The enemy hit you with the *uppercut*

It's now 2-1

Where do you possibly go from here?

No victory seems to be in sight

You no longer feel the need to fight

Again that little voice tells you

"Try going into **Round 4**"

Your body is getting weak and sore and you're mentality breaking down

Coming into this round in a *Full Crouch* Your hands are up to block the punch that's coming your way

But your opponent comes strong with more than one to the face

Bob and Weave, and do a Peek-a-boo

To get to what you think is prepared for you

And yet you don't know exactly what is meant for you because again, it's confusion

You see no end in sight and the more foot work you do, the more *punches* come to you

You no longer see the ***purpose*** of doing anything, as for you feel defeated

Another *uppercut and jab* is what he gave me

Stuck in the ***phase of disparity***

The score is 3-1; your opponent leads the match

Opening **Round 5**

You really want to throw in the towel

Time and time again that's just what you felt within

Nothing comes your way except *Cross-hooks* and pain

Plus the *Jab of temptation* is plain

Temptation leads you down this path

The *uppercut* is the enemy's wrath

Your opponent now has you where he wants you

Punching and jabbing you in the corner

And then your opponent released you before getting counted out

You fall out to the mat, barely making the count

It's 4-1, all because of **Temptation and doubt**

Man, this fight seems pointless
Right ?
The opponent has control
Taking out of your soul the passion that you once had, the stamina is no longer
Endurance was long gone; might as well call it off

Suddenly that voice that you once heard comes again
Seeing visions of Angels within your midst
Your Coach begins to give you that pep talk

Round 6
You have the best defense
Coming out of the corner feeling fresh and new
You throw the *jab* that once stabbed you
Your opponent doesn't know what happened because it came so quick; he then tried to *bob* but didn't last
With that "I can do" attitude
You threw that *Overhand Right* combined with a *jab*
Perplexed at the combination of **Faith**
The enemy got a taste
Your opponent tries to move to the *left but you move to the right*; he tries to throw that *Left Hook* but you throw the *Right*
You follow up with that *Check-Hook* and knock him out nice

Round 7
lasts a little longer because your mentality has gotten stronger and that's what your opponent is after
Your foot-work is fancier and staying out of corners

Now you're building that **Relationship** with your Coach
The conditioning was there, but the ***discipline*** wasn't
You weren't looking to believe
The opponent doesn't know what to do his tactics aren't coming through
Parry-Blocking the enemy's best defense
You throw him in the corner and through *punch after punch*
Clinching the opponent with all your might
You just raised that score 3-4

Eight Rounds in
A feeling of no end
This is the toughest fight you've ever been in
But something tells you to go on
This is the toughest fight you've ever been in
But something tells you to go on
Suddenly, you think about your Coach and all that He says
He constantly reminds you that He's always training you
Even when you turned your back on Him
Because you now have **Faith and Relationship**
He still shows you love
Your opponent is weakened because of your stable mind
With your hands up
Again you *block that Punch of hate*
Instead, you defend it with a *Cross-arm of Love*
Bobbing and weaving once again
From one side to the other
Your opponent gets tired and passes out
With **Love and Compassion** from the Coach to you
Tying the score to 4-4

Round 9 It's crunch time
Gloves still on
Shoes are tight
Get some fresh water in your mouth and spit it out
Look up to Coach and say, "I'm alright"
You look ahead and see the fight, wish it would end
Coach is saying, "Trust me until no end"
Trust me for I am training you
"I'm giving you all the techniques to sustain you
The bell has rung
The opponent is barely up
In your *full Stance* you hit him with that *Uppercut of Hope*
The opponent once again wasn't expecting it
You get the adrenaline once more
You've found the strength to endure
The enemy doesn't know what to do
He no longer has this hold on you; he tries to throw something back. You hit him with that *Right-Arm Hook of Trust*
Then followed it up with the *Overhead Right of Faith*; he tried to swing and you ducked
You hit him with the combo because you've found your **Purpose**
Rights and Lefts and Rights again
You've established this Round the opponent can't win

Wow **Round 10**
And it seems to be coming to an end
You've got that flow and feel like **Muhammad-Ali** in his prime
Coach tells you to take it slow and save energy
But you just can't sit still. You gain that over-confidence

Your opponent looks pretty beat up and your **Prideful** thoughts consume you again

So you get up in your *Full Stance* and begin:

You hit him with a *right*; he hits you right back

You get him with a *left*; he gets you in the chest

*Knocking t*he wind out of you

The techniques that you used no longer work

You've gotten too **Comfortable** and the opponent knows

Because of your comfortability, the enemy has stolen again

Tied once again

Shocked and unenthused

Meanwhile, your opponent is grinning ear to ear

Coach tried to tell you, but pride took over

Round 11

You know is a little different

Instead of physical, you use mental tactics

You're more cautious

Your opponent has already calculated your moves from *punch to punch*

You conserve your energy

Instead of throwing *punches* you, go back to the basics

And just *Bob and weave* out of it

Your opponent comes at you with a *jab* from round 1

Then tries the same from round 2

You just continued to *duck* under and under again

Step back, he tried to hit your ***identity***

But because you know your ***purpose***

You weaved and threw the Jab of Faith; he then tried to throw a combo of temptation and comfort

And yet you got 'em with the *Overhand* of knowing your

atmospheric principalities
The opponent feels weak and passes out
Giving you peaceful light

Round 12

Coach reminds you of all your conditioning and training
Your opponent appears to be sluggish
That hold of physical or mental abuse is no longer there; he steps in to throw a *punch* and you matched him back
You put up your arms to *block*; he tries to get you in a *head lock*
You spin out and throw out a *jab*; he gets you in the ribs
Coach sees what's happening and throws out His protecting words
The opponent comes strong with *jabs and punches* because he's jealous of your **relationship**
And he thinks he has you until Coach gets in on it
Jab after punch and *punch after jab*
The opponent gets mad; he can no longer duck because he alone gets stuck
Can't quite understand where you found the power and strength
But it was all within **Coach's Grace**
So *Bob and weave* and *duck and dive*
This is the ultimate fight for life
And when he least expects it
You hit 'em with the *K.O. punch* of **Salvation**
Coach graciously smiles
For he knew you had the power; the *count goes to 10*
The opponent is out for the count
Coach gets in the Ring and the crowd shouts
Victory has at last been yours making the score 7-5
Through this long battle of yours Coach already prepared you for your enemy's demise

This Boxing Ring of Life will bring you through trials and tribulations but Coach will never leave you hopeless
You fight through all the **Temptations and Principalities** that the enemy will put in your way
God's Salvation has the final say
Victory means Victor, so let the enemy be the victim in your Boxing Ring

Made in the USA
Middletown, DE
21 January 2022